Greta Thunberg Coming to America

Narrated By
Acie Cargill

ISBN: 9781690053644

Imprint: Independently published

Formatted - Brenda Van Niekerk

brenda@triomarketers.com

Website Design - Brenda Van Niekerk

http://triomarketers.com

Synopsis

For one thing, it will be difficult to match the carbon-free method she used to get to the Western Hemisphere on that racing sailboat. Eventually she can probably get a ride back to her home in Sweden by a similar method, but for awhile she will probably remain active here in the Americas which includes the many states of the Union, Canada, Mexico, Central America and the countries of South America that desperately need her inspiration. Coming up next year is a world environmental conference to be held in Chile. She has said she wants to attend it. So that gives her a year to expand her burgeoning following of teen environmental activists.

She is an inspiration. American countries are already the worst environmental offenders, especially the United States. Under its present leadership, it does not seem likely that there will be a mass demand for climate action and climate justice by people who have the power to do it. But that may change if there are a hundred million teens marching under the leadership of their quiet inspiration, Greta Thunberg.

This book contains some of her most famous speeches in Europe before she came to the US. Also many of her internet followers reacting to her daily reports at sea, and her actual daily log on the voyage.

About the Author

Acie Cargill is a poet, a songwriter, and a prose writer. He studied poetry with USA Poet Laureate Mark Strand and Illinois Poet Laureate Gwendolyn Brooks. He studied novel writing with Thomas Berger, who wrote Little Big Man (that Arthur Penn made into a movie with Dustin Hoffman in the lead role). Cargill also studied journalism with instructor Jean Daily. His work is a synthesis of all these styles.

He is a member of American Mensa and formerly Edited the Mensa Journal of Poetry. He also is a member of the Grammy Association, and The US Quill and Scroll Society.

Cargill is a vegetarian, a former holistic physician, a musical performer on a variety of instruments, an environmental activist, a lecturer, medical reviewer, a lover, and a seer.

Website

http://aciecargill.com

Contact

aciecargill@gmail.com

Other Books Written by the Author:

Puerto Rico

Aberrations

Chronicles

Terrorism

Modern Love

Ends and odds

Illiana: The Border Area Between Illinois and Indiana

Pullman

Che and Fidel - A Reading Play of the Cuban Revolution

Celia Sanchez - A Play of the Cuban Revolution

Paschke - A Play

Gwendolyn Brooks: A Play

Rasputin - A Play

Nietzsche - A Play

Bob Dylan, The Early Years - A Musical Play

Michael Jackson - A Play

Einstein - A Biographical Play

El Chapo - A Play In 3 Acts

Raisins and Roaches - A Three Month Diary of a Crack Addict

Susan B. Anthony - A Biographical Play

Kankakee

Harriet Tubman - A Biographical Play

Tesla - A Biographical Play

Vegan Saint - A Play in 3 Acts

Martin Luther King, Jr - A Play

Great Migration: A Play in 3 Acts

George Pullman - A Play in Three Acts

Frederick Douglass - A Biographical Play

Freud - A Biographical Play in 3 Acts

The Underground Railroad - An Educational Play

Payton, Jordan, Ali - A Biographical Play

Mr. Nobody - A Play

The Kid From Left Field - A Play

Puerto Rico, A Dream of Independence - A Play in 3 Acts

Crack Madness - A Monologue Play

Johnny Appleseed - A Family Play

Dr. Jekll and Mr. Hyde - A Modernized Play

Obama - Obama - A Play In 3 Acts

Will Rogers - A Biographical Monologue

Merle Haggard - A Biographical Monologue

Mother Teresa - A Biographical Monologue

Gwendolyn Brooks - A Biographical Monologue

Love Life of Susan B. Anthony - A Monologue Play

Sojourner Truth - A Biographical Monologue plus Narrator

Harriet Tubman and The Underground Railroad - A Play

Helen Keller, Words and Wisdom - A Biographical Play

Eugene Debs and the 1894 Pullman Strike - A Play

The Rising - A Play

Walt Disney - A Biographical One Act Play

The Experiments of Dr. Victor Frankenstein - A Play - Based on the novel by Mary Shelley

Karl Marx - A One Act Play

Martin Luther at The Diet of Worms - A One Act Play

Martin Luther King: Monologue and Narrator Play

Frederick Douglass - Monologue and Narrator Play

Kaepernick - A One Act Play

Settling South Holland - A Play In 2 Acts

Kaepernick - A Full-Length Play

My Son Died From An Overdose - A Play

Overdose - A One Act Play

Always a Marine First

Erotic Muslim Polygamy

George Dolton's Bridge to Freedom Underground Railroad - A One-Act Play

Greta Thunberg - A One-Act Play About Climate Change

A Brief History of the Philippines

Goat With No Horns - Voodoo Cannibals in Haiti

Johnny Cash - Monologue Play

Muhammad Words Of Wisdom

Jesus Words Of Wisdom

Bob Hope - Biographical Monologue

The Cargills of Graves County, Ky

Keith Raniere and the NXIVM Sex Club

Words of Wisdom – Native Americans, Ancient Greeks, Buddha and African-Americans

Words of Wisdom – Mark Twain, Benjamin Franklin, Shakespeare and Solomon

The Trial of Eddie Gallagher, Navy SEAL

Climate Crisis - A Plan to Prevent Future Flooding

Yukio Mishima - Life, Death, Hara Kiri

My "Cuzin Willie" Nelson - A Biographical Monologue

The World's Most Amazing Person, Elon Musk

The Beatles: Early Years - A One-Act Play

Red Summer Race Riot Chicago 1919 - Eyewitnesses John Harris and Ida B. Wells

Jeffrey Epstein - Illicit Kicks and Retribution

Gandhi - A Brief Biography

Jeffrey Epstein - Death Controversy

Table of Contents

1. Flyt Skamen (flight shame)

Greta Thunberg is a proponent of avoiding all plane flight because of the huge carbon emissions generated. One flight is like a family car for a year. She takes trains, or electric cars or buses to get around to her many speaking engagements in Europe. She has an ally in the United States with congresswoman Alexandria Ocasio-Cortez who also avoids plane flights unless absolutely necessary because of the carbon emissions.

So when Greta was invited to speak at the United Nations climate crisis program in September of 2019 she had to find a low carbon way to get to the United States. Her plight attracted the attention of the skipper of a modern sailing race boat that used electric motors for mooring and emergencies. The electric motors were charged by solar panels and underwater turbines that also provided power for a minimum amount of electric lighting and internet connectivity. The vessel was captained by veteran race sailor Boris Herrmann and team founder Pierre Casiraghi, the grandson of Prince Rainier and Grace Kelly of Monaco. The name of the ship is the Malizia II.

Since the ship is a racing vehicle it is basically stripped of any comforts. The two sailors alternate on one bunk, Greta has one, her father Svante has one and their videographer has the other. There are no cooking facilities, so they ate freeze dried meals stored in sealed plastic. There is no toilet or shower. They use plastic buckets for waste disposal and empty it overboard into the sea. Their drinking water is provided by a small desalination plant powered by the ships small electricity generation from solar and water turbines.

Ms. Thunberg wore black sailing gear and boots for what will be a roughly two-week journey at sea. "Unite Behind the Science," read the logo on her suit and on the mainsail, raised against a gray sky. Her hair was tied back in a signature braid. In a particularly acute challenge for a teenager with more than 871,000 Twitter followers, she will not have much access to the internet. Ms. Thunberg will have to read by headlamp.

She has never done anything like this before. She said she was looking forward to being without the familiar luxuries, to "being so limited." She acknowledged being a bit nervous. "Whether it's seasickness or homesickness or just anxiety or I don't know," she said. "I don't know how tough this journey will be."

Also, she said, she will really miss her two dogs.

She has packed many books (she is currently reading "Quiet," a book about introverts, like her); eight writing journals, some partly filled; and boxes of freeze-dried vegan meals. (Ms. Thunberg stopped eating meat a few years ago, because of the emissions associated with animal protein.)

The ride is rough on the 60-foot sailboat and they feared Greta and her father and cameraman would suffer sea sickness especially in the rough seas cause by an Atlantic storm. The boat was really rocking, but everyone survived even though they might have been a little uncomfortable. The two sailors had made the Atlantic crossing other times and were not bothered by the rough weather. Anyway, they left from Plymouth in England and arrived at New York 15 days later. That was fast sailing averaging around 25 miles per hour.

There is a satellite phone on board, so she planned to send some pictures and text messages from her voyage to friends who will upload them on her social media accounts. She had notified her New York followers on social media when she would be arriving and there was an excited crowd waiting to welcome her and cheer for her arrival.

This was Greta's first sea voyage, but being Swedish, her ancestors were seafaring people, so she took to the experience well and undaunted. It was important that she travelled that way because she recommends others to do it and would not have been a good example if she flew all that way. Greta is the face of the green revolution combatting climate change and everything she does is well observed and widely reported.

2. Meghan Markle comments about Greta before she left England

One of Meghan Markle's handpicked "Forces for Change" just proved again how she's living up to the title. When Meghan chose 15 women making a difference in the world to grace the cover of her guest-edited September issue of British Vogue, 16-year-old climate and environmentalist activist Greta Thunberg made the exclusive list.

Meghan first hinted she was a big fan of the Swedish teen when she and Prince Harry followed her on Instagram in July, highlighting her while championing environmental causes. And on Wednesday, Thunberg sailed past the Statue of Liberty and the Freedom Tower into New York Harbor to prove a point about environmentally friendly travel.

Thunberg was on her way to speak at the UN Climate Action Summit on September 23, traveling on a zero-emissions sailboat to reduce the environmental impact of her journey.

"I would love not to have to do this and just go to school, but... I want to make a difference," Thunberg said at a press conference after docking. Thunberg was named one of Time's Most Influential Teens of 2018 and nominated for a 2019 Nobel Peace Prize for her efforts to halt climate change.

3. Greta's Sailing Log

Test sailing off the English coast today!

The weather forecast looks good, we are due to leave Plymouth as planned, at 15.00 GMT

We are on our way!

Leaving Plymouth and heading for New York. Follow our journey here on Facebook and track us live through this link https://www.borisherrmannracing.com/a-race-we-must-win/

Day 2. 100 nautical miles west of Cape Finisterre. A very bumpy night but I slept surprisingly well. Some dolphins showed up and swam along the boat last nigh

Day 3 School strike week 52.

Pos 47 degrees 17 minutes north and 13 degrees

Day 4. Pos 46° 20' N 015° 46' W

Eating and sleeping well and no sea sickness so far. Life on Malizia II is like camping on a roller coaster!

Day 5. Pos 42° 55' N 022° 12' W. A sunny day with nice winds. BorisHerrmannRacing and Team Malizia

Day 6. Sunshine sailing north of the Azores

One year ago I started school striking for the climate outside the Swedish parliament, simply because something had to be done. Since then I have continued every Friday alongside millions of others. And we will go on for as long as it takes. #FridaysForFuture #SchoolStrike4climate

Day 7. About halfway across the Atlantic Ocean. Very pleasant conditions.

Day 8. 42° 25′ N 39° 27′ W. At sea you really loose sense of time and you can't separate the days. You sleep, eat, look at the ocean.

Malizia 2 is fitted with solar panels and hydro generators making it one of the very few ships in the world allowing trips like this to be emission free.

Malizia 2 also has an onboard lab to measure ocean surface CO_2 and water temperature in cooperation with Max Planck institute.

Day 11. Very bumpy and wet, south of Newfoundland.

Day 12. We are getting closer to the North American mainland. Rough conditions, but downwind sailing.

Strong winds are pushing us west. We expect to arrive at North Cove Marina in Manhattan, New York sometime Tuesday afternoon or evening.

Day 13. Rough seas south of Nova Scotia. But conditions closer to New York will be slower than predicted and weather update suggests Wednesday arrival - an updated ETA will come as we near the coast.

Day 14. 119 miles from Manhattan. Very light winds south of Long Island.

Land!! The lights of Long Island and New York City ahead.

We have anchored off Coney Island - clearing customs and immigration. We will come ashore at North Cove Marina earliest 14:45 tide allowing.

Sailing into New York.

Home Sweet Home since 14 days. Soon last evening onboard Malizia II. Tomorrow we reach New York.

Finally here. Thank you everyone who came to see me off in Plymouth, and everyone who welcomed me in New York! Now I'm going to rest for a few days, and on Friday I'm going to participate in the strike outside the UN.

4. Arriving in New York

Sailing with Greta on the 60-foot Malizia II racing yacht (equipped with solar panels and underwater turbines) was Grace Kelly's grandson, Pierre Casiraghi. Pierre acted as skipper on the two-week journey across the Atlantic Ocean. The son of Princess Caroline of Monaco congratulated Greta for making the cross-ocean journey with such grace.

"I am full of praise for Thunberg's courage and determination; her attitude on board Malizia II was exemplary despite the extreme living conditions," he said after arriving in New York. "I would like to thank everyone in the Malizia team and the Prince Albert II of Monaco Foundation. It was a very emotional moment sailing past the Statue of Liberty, and I thank everyone for all the support we received during this amazing adventure crossing the Atlantic."

Pierre, who owns the carbon-neutral boat, said that he reached out to Greta after hearing she was looking for a sustainable way to travel to the climate summit to be held in New York. "They had a lot of questions and they had been exploring different kinds of boats to get across," he said. "We explained this is a racing boat, that there is little comfort on the boat, but she seems fine with that."

Arriving in NYC, Thunberg was greeted by an enormous chanting crowd — and at least one billboard boat, which, according to was flashing a message about climate change, but still. Regardless, Thunberg's supporters were thrilled to see her.

"I think that she's a wonderful person and she'll help so much with climate change and we might stand a chance if we could actually fix this democracy we're living in," Ésme Ruiz, 8, told Hogan.

"I'm just so excited," 17-year-old Arden Astin, a fellow boat-dweller, agreed. "I'm so happy to see this happening... it's like the best thing going on in the world right now." Another Astin, 8-year-old Riley, echoed that sentiment. "I'm very glad that Greta has come to help us recognize that the world really means something, and that all the animals and sea life are depending on us," Riley told Hogan. "It's very tragic for the world to be experiencing this."

After disembarking on Wednesday, Thunberg gave a brief press conference in Downtown Manhattan. "The war against nature must end," she said, adding that — once she gets some rest and a bath — she'll be joining a student protest on Friday. "My message to all the activists: Just keep going. I know it may seem impossible at times."

Several young people said that they had first learned about Thunberg from YouTube, but had been motivated to act because they've learned how climate change is impacting people around the world.

Olivia Wohlgemuth, a 16-year-old student at LaGuardia High School, said that while she's worried about the future, protesting to raise awareness gives her hope. "I always feel so hopeful at protests. Climate change can be so bleak and action can be an antidote to that," Wohlgemuth said.

.Several teenagers, including 15-year-old Dwight School student Alessandro Dal Bon, said that Thunberg had been the inspiration for them to get involved with climate activism.

"She's not afraid of anyone. She's not afraid of the politicians, she's not afraid of the businessmen. She just wants to get her message out there. And she's willing to do anything for that. She's willing to cross the Atlantic Ocean for 15 days on a small boat to do that. That just shows you how determined she is," Dal Bon says.

Thunberg thanked the sailboat's team and said that the trip had been "surprisingly good," noting that she hadn't gotten seasick. She said that she would miss feeling "disconnected" from the world during the journey.

"To just sit, literally sit for hours, and just stare at the ocean not doing anything. That was great. And I'm going to miss that a lot," Thunberg said. "And of course, to be in this wilderness, the ocean, and to see the beauty of it. "

Thunberg seemed a little weary from her journey, but spoke forcefully about climate change. While she doesn't expect everyone to cross the Atlantic Ocean in a boat like she did, she said that she believes it's time for people to come together to fight climate change.

Thunberg said that while she's hoping to spread the word about climate change, one person isn't the primary focus of her message—President Donald Trump. "My message for him is just listen to the science, and he obviously doesn't do that. As I always say to this question, if no one has been able to convince him about the climate crisis, the urgency, why should I be able to do that?" Thunberg said.

Here is her short arrival speech in New York that day' "The climate and environmental crisis is a global crisis and it is the biggest crisis that humanity has ever faced and if we don't work together and cooperate despite our differences then we will fail. We need to stand together and support each other and take action because otherwise, it might be too late. Let's not wait any longer. Let's do it now."

5. Greta's First strike in United States Aug 30, 2019 in New York

Greta was seated with her famous Skolestrejk for Klimatet (schoolstrike for climate) sign. This time she is in New York and she is surrounded by hundreds od devoted teenagers. Most are carrying hand-written signs on cardboard sort of like Greta's. They are chanting the slogans they use in their demonstrations and all of them seem to know them. The place is filled with Greta's admirers and it is an honor to sit close to her. Greta chooses her spot and the others follow.

"Stop denying. The Earth is dying."

Youthful smiling faces. No makeup. Plain hairstyles. Their concern is for the safety of the planet, not being artificially beautiful as an attraction device. They are just not into that. They are into lowering the temperature of the earth and at least preventing any raising of the temperature which would indicate increased greenhouse gases, especially CO_2 in the atmosphere.

"The levels are rising And so are we"

We stand united. You across the country and across the wall are coming together. This climate crisis should not be placed on our generation's shoulders. Nothing is being done by world leaders and people in power. Climate change is already affecting millions of lives. I cannot understand why world leaders are not doing anything

"No more coal and no more oil. Keep the carbon in the soil."

6. Getting Ready for the UN Summit

In August last year, teen activist Greta Thunberg began a solitary climate protest on the steps of the Swedish parliament every Friday. In January this year, teen activist Alexandria Villasenor began a solitary climate protest in front of the United Nations in New York. This Friday, their worlds' collided.

Thunberg arrived in New York via a carbon-free racing boat trip across the Atlantic. On Friday, Villaseñor sat on her customary bench. A half hour later, Thunberg took up a spot in Ralph Bunche Park four blocks away. Villaseñor walked to meet her and a large group of American youth activists who shared their stories of what it means to be the ones who will live with adults' decisions today.

"What do you want?

Climate Justice

When do we want it?

Now

What if we don't get it?

Shut it down"

Large groups of teens chanting the slogans of their movement. It is the future. Greta is the mostly silent figurehead. She is always in the center of the action, but she usually doesn't speak. She has Asperger's Syndrome and she doesn't talk for long periods, In fact in her honor the teens have long periods of silence while they hold up their hands in peace signs. They go a long time in absolute silence. Just like Greta does. They dress similar to her and many have plain unadorned hair arrangements like Greta does also. She does smile at the people around her. That day there was a pretty teen leader sitting by her that saw to it that Greta was always comfortable.

"We are unstoppable. A better world is possible."

The demonstrators have many chants and it seems like everyone knows them. They love calling out those slogans of the environment. Especially now in Greta's honor. They know what she went through to get there. Two weeks on a rough racing sailboat crossing the Atlantic Ocean. Sometimes storms. No toilets. No shower. No stove or refrigerator. Minimal lighting. But she was able to satisfy her following with messages to her social media accounts including Facebook and Twitter.

Thunberg became an international sensation for her direct and plain statements on the climate crisis to world leaders. Her words have helped build a movement brought 1.6 million young adults into the streets in March for a global strike. And now, with the United Nations poised to hold a massive climate summit on September 23, the youth are gearing up to mobilize again. Friday, September 20 is slated to be another global day of action. Thunberg will be striking here in the U.S. ahead of speaking at the United Nations on Monday. So consider this Friday's strike a warm up.

And if the warm up is any indication, the coming strikes will be major. Youth activists crowded around Thunberg, chanting about climate justice and their goals for striking. A number of activists stood up and gave testimony for why they strike and how the world had failed them as media jostled to capture the historic moment. It was chaos at times. The soft-spoken Thunberg who had been in the United States for less than 48 hours seemed exhausted.

Yet she stayed in solidarity with the protestors while they shared their stories about the climate crisis. And they made it clear they understand the risks and they hate the lies they've been dealt by adults.

"The climate crisis follows you. It is affecting everyone, everywhere," Xiya Bastida, a 17 year old activist who moved to the U.S. from Mexico, said to the assembled crowd. "We cannot live in a world where a 16-year-old has to cross the Atlantic to get you to pay attention." "They have chosen money over our future," Villaseñor said. "We should not have to worry about that."

Those worrisome choices continued in the U.S. this week as the Trump administration announced it was rolling back a key methane rule, just a month after the hottest month in recorded history. It's an uphill battle activists face, especially as time to address the climate crisis dwindles.

Greta is here now in the US and she is taking the year off from her schooling to travel around to meet, organize, and promote protests against the way the Unites States ignores the precautions recommended by the Paris agreements for environmental health.

A year from now she wants to go to a conference in Chili on the environment, but until then she will be pushing for climate justice her in North America.

She is very concerned about the terrible fires in the Amazon rain forests. She probably will be making stops eventually in Brazil and Bolivia at least. We have a global crisis and she is energetic and willing to promote her agenda in as many places as possible. The teens love her. She is the biggest thing now in many of their lives and the movement is going to grow and grow as she travels around the United States and Canada.

She is sort of a Joan of Arc type of figurehead and she does give long speeches occasionally and she likes to answer questions in press conference type settings. She is often quiet, but she is always paying attention to her surroundings and activities near her and she likes publicity for her cause.

7. Climate Strike in New York Sept 20, 2019

Volunteer with us to create art and other important resources for the Climate Strike. Sign up to attend the art build on Friday, August 30 or Saturday, August 31.

Not in New York?

Click here to go back to the national map of US Climate Strike events.

On September 20, three days before the UN Climate Summit in NYC, young people and adults will strike all across the US and the world to demand transformative action be taken to address the climate crisis. Millions of us will take to the streets globally to demand justice for our present and a right to a future.

In New York, we will march and rally to demand real action by our elected officials and world leaders. We will gather at Foley Square and then take to the streets to march to Battery Park. The event will conclude with speakers and performers, including Fridays For Future movement starter Greta Thunberg and NY-based youth leaders .

RSVP now to #StrikeWithUs.

Visit the Climate Strike NYC website to learn more.

Schedule:

12:00 PM - Assemble at Foley Square

1:00 PM - March to Battery Park

2:30 - 5:00 PM - Rally at Battery Park

8. What about communicating the science?

Young climate justice activists don't have time for skeptics. "Our future is going to be the most affected if we don't do something right now," 17-year-old environmental activist Xiye Bastida says.

Up until recently, their movement has been completely youth led. But Bastida says, for voting power and "intergenerational cooperation and collaboration," the teens are turning to adults for help. Yet, it's important to note their movement exists because of youth organizing. Student walk-outs across Europe began in 2018. Since then, they have put together massive global strikes, which included participation from more than 100 countries.

On Friday, hundreds of teens joined Swedish environmental activist, 16-year-old Greta Thunberg, protesting outside of the U.N. headquarters in New York City, insisting world leaders take action. Thunberg said she traveled to the U.S. for this demonstration to get "a concrete plan, not just nice words" from lawmakers.

"Our global demand is that the temperature stays below 1.5 degrees of warming," Bastida says. That leaves 10 years and five months to curb carbon emissions if humans want to meet that goal, she says.

As Bastida prepares for the September 20th strike — which she says will be "the biggest global climate strike yet" — she reflects on the overwhelming support from the previous two events. "On March 15th, we had our first global climate strike with 1.6 million students," she says. "On May 24, we heard we had our second one with 1.9 million students."

For organizers involved in the worldwide demonstrations, getting the message across is key. In July, Thunberg said that spreading information about climate change is one of the most practical actions one can take.

"The most important thing you can do now as an individual is to try to read all these things that no one wants to read," Thunberg said. "And I know that is very boring, and that is why this information needs to become more available and then put pressure on the people in power."

Bastida says this is exactly what her and other climate leaders are doing — being as informed as they can. "We read the reports. We know about the IPCC. We know that we have 415 parts per million of carbon in the atmosphere and that the safe amount is 350 parts per million," she says. "So we can communicate [to] you the science. We haven't done the science ourselves, but we are messengers because we need to act now."

9. Greta and Alexandria attacked by right wing climate deniers

Climate change may not seem like a gendered issue, but leave it to conservatives to inject sexism into everything they do.

That much was made evident when the right-wing Media Research Center tweeted out a video of Rep. Alexandria Ocasio-Cortez, D-N.Y., talking about the need for rapid decarbonization to prevent catastrophic environmental changes due to climate change. This video, which is as an indictment of Ocasio-Cortez's intelligence. Despite the heavy-handed presentation, if a viewer actually listens to what Ocasio-Cortez is saying, it's quite clear she's making a cogent and intelligent case, and understands the actual scientific evidence far better than her detractors.

Ocasio-Cortez tweeted out a warm welcome to Greta Thunberg, the 16-year-old Swedish climate activist, who arrived in New York Wednesday for a speech at the United Nations. Unfortunately, Thunberg was also greeted by a wave of misogynist nastiness, largely coming from allegedly grown men in both Europe and the United States. The attacks on Thunberg were in the same vein as those on Ocasio-Cortez, accusing her of being too stupid to know what she's talking about and denying that her voice is one worth honoring. A writer for the conservative Washington Examiner claimed that Thunberg is a victim of "child abuse" and that her mother "pimps their kid out," explicitly drawing a line between forced sex work and climate activism.

Right-wingers to lean heavily on sexist stereotypes to dismiss serious, evidence-based and morally urgent crusades to do something about climate change before it's too late. Now they're shifting those same attacks onto women who are increasingly becoming the face of climate change activism.

But no matter who the right attacks, the premise remains the same: Environmentalists are female and or effeminate, and therefore can be dismissed out of hand as stupid or crazy or driven by irrational emotion — in other words, not worth listening to. Women are so worthless in their eyes, it appears, that no amount of evidence will ever make women's arguments hold merit.

These kinds attacks have no basis in fact. Thunberg's views on climate change align with those of better than 97% of climate scientists. Thunberg is no helpless puppet, but a sharp and remarkably passionate young person who has sparked an international youth movement of climate activism with millions of participants. In order to give weight to these attacks, these critics rely on stereotypes painting women, especially young women, as infantile and idiotic. Without this kind of misogyny, they'd have nothing. "While these examples might feel like mere coincidence to some," Martin Gelin argues "the idea that white men would lead the attacks on Greta Thunberg is consistent with a growing body of research linking gender reactionaries to climate-denialism."

Indeed, the evidence Gelin cites shows that sexism is probably fueling climate denialism. Researchers Jonas Anshelm and Martin Hultman of Chalmers found that sexists saw climate change activism as part of a larger group of social changes — including feminism — that threatens "a certain kind of modern industrial society built and dominated by their form of masculinity." Other research shows that American men find environmentalism to be inherently feminine and therefore emasculating, and view being deliberately anti-environmental as a way to feel more masculine.

10. Input from Mom and Dad, Malena and Svante

Food is partly how all this began. Thunberg is even smaller than you might suspect, child-slight and not yet five foot. She looks more like 12 than 16. This is the result of a bout of severe depression when she was eleven and a serious eating disorder that followed. In two months, she lost ten kilos and stopped talking.

Scenes From The Heart, the family's memoir, mostly written by her mother, details their trauma. It's a Tuesday morning in November 2014. Two months earlier, Thunberg had stopped eating. And so now, by the dining table, an A3 sheet hangs on the wall, on which they note what Thunberg eats, how much, how long it takes and how many bites it requires. They've begged, pleaded, bribed, cried and threatened, but have found a sort of a stealth surveillance the best method. After breakfast they write, "Breakfast: 1/3 banana. Time: 53 minutes."

Time passes like this for a while. Hospital appointments and tests, counselling sessions. On the A3 sheet they write things like "A banana. 25 minutes" and "An avocado with 25 grams of rice. 30 minutes." Finally, she is given sertraline for her depression and the long road back begins. The weight loss stops. They start to write things like "Salmon" and "Croquettes" on the wall.

By the time she returns to school, there's hope. But while Thunberg has always been a smart child – she has a photographic memory, can recite every world capital, can even name all the elements, though she struggles with the pronunciation – it's the other children that prove to be the problem.

She finds herself bullied relentlessly. The children can sense she's different and that difference is reason enough. But her parents only discover it when her father, Svante, takes her to the school Christmas party and finds that, even with him standing next to her, her classmates openly point and laugh.

It's clear from their book Scenes From The Heart that both parents have input into her speeches. When Thunberg addressed the World Economic Forum in Davos on 25 January, she began with the words, "Our house is on fire. I am here to say, 'Our house is on fire.'" We are less than 12 years away, she pointed out, from being unable to undo our mistakes. At a minimum, we need to reduce our CO_2 emissions by at least 50 per cent immediately. She ended with this plea for urgency: "I want you to act as you would in a crisis. I want you to act as if our house is on fire. Because it is."

In the 72nd part of Scenes From The Heart, about a time before Greta has embarked on her school strike for climate, Malena details her husband's phone call with a publisher who would like them to write a "hopeful" book on the environment. They had been in London on a family holiday and were making the long journey back by road to Stockholm in their electric car. While on the call, Svante thinks of a fact Greta told him: that a single plane trip can nullify 20 years of recycling.

"In the current situation we do not think hope is what we need the most," Svante tells the publisher. "That would mean continuing to look away. If your house is on fire, you don't sit down at the kitchen table first and tell your family how pretty everything will be when you rebuild."

The publisher says they'll call back, but of course they don't. On the journey, they soon find themselves surrounded by other vehicles and, for the second time in 15 years, Svante starts to cry, Malena writes, "Because there, surrounded by 50 billion trucks, highways and BMWs, he understands it does not matter how many solar cells we place on the roof or how much we cheer or inspire each other. What we need is a revolution. The largest in human history. And we need it now."

Over the Christmas break from school, Greta tells them about the bullying she gets from the other children maybe because she is so small (under 5 feet), but in an amused way, as if it happened to someone else or she's recounting scenes from a high-school film. The beatings, the ambushes, the systematic exclusion, the way she hid in the girls' toilets until she was forced into the schoolyard. The school even blames her for it, telling her parents that several students have said Thunberg behaves strangely, talking too quietly and never saying hello.

"I do not want friends," she tells her mother simply. "All children are mean."

Not long after, at the Stockholm Centre For Eating Disorders, Thunberg's physical condition has finally reached a level that allows them to perform neuropsychiatric testing.

She is diagnosed with Asperger's, high-functioning autism and obsessive -compulsive disorder. To her mother, though, it's a diagnosis that comes with relief rather than worry; a feeling that the woods have cleared and finally there is a path to follow.

And she realises something else too. It's spring now and as she walks her daughter home something wondrous occurs to her: it is the first time she can remember that she didn't have to worry about the calories her daughter is burning.

Greta has said her recovery from depression was aided by her focus on the climate. In the weeks and months she was off school, she spoke to her parents about her worries and fears and the thing she kept coming back to was the environment.

"We started talking because we had nothing else to do. And it felt good to get that off my chest," she said. She showed her parents "pictures, graphs and films, articles and reports. After a while they started listening to what I actually said. That's when I kind of realised I could make a difference."

Greta – still, deliberate, no fan of small talk – said, "I write all of my own speeches," but also allowed, "I ask people for input." Her father, she says, "sometimes tries to tone them down a little. He's a bit worried I might say something bad, which I'm already doing, but he's still scared."

She remembers addressing the secretary-general of the United Nations once, "and I was saying, 'What's the point of going to school if we don't have a future?' And he [Greta's father] was so worried, as he hadn't seen my speech before. He was like, 'You can't say that to the secretary-general!' I did erase it and printed it without it. But then I remembered it during the speech and added it while I was speaking, so he couldn't say anything about it."

11. Greta in the Americas

For one thing, it will be difficult to match the carbon-free method she used to get to the Western Hemisphere on that racing sailboat. Eventually she can probably get a ride back to her home in Sweden by a similar method, but for awhile she will probably remain active here in the Americas which includes the many states of the Union, Canada, Mexico, Central America and the countries of South America that desperately need her inspiration. Coming up next year is a world environmental conference to be held in Chile. She has said she wants to attend it. So that gives her a year to expand her burgeoning following of teen environmental activists.

She is an inspiration. American countries are already the worst environmental offenders, especially the United States. Under its present leadership, it does not seem likely that there will be a mass demand for climate action and climate justice by people who have the power to do it. But that may change if there are a hundred million teens marching under the leadership of their quiet inspiration, Gre ta Thunberg,

She may make strong allies like Ocasio-Cortez in the Hispanic communities and Kaepernick with the African Americans, although at present, both of those leaders seem to be especially interested in human rights and equal social justice for their followers. But after a year of Greta speaking and inspiring protests by the teens who are enthralled by her, more and more people will realize the importance of a green revolution. Does that include the Republican political leaderships? Maybe not, but maybe her influence can cause a change in the balance of power.

Maybe these teens do not have actual voting power, but they are going to be very influential. If nothing else, they will certainly make more people aware of the danger of continuing with the environmental destruction. This is their future world. They will be demanding that changes be made. If the politicians continue to ignore the protests, eventually they will be voted out of power. It might take a few more years, but the teen green revolution is not going to go away. They will carry their ideas and their promotions with them all their lives. Yes, it is going to be starting this year with Greta in the United States travelling around and spreading her awareness.

She doesn't speak much at her demonstrations and protests, but she inspires others to speak and chant the slogans. Even if she is quiet, her teen followers are happy she is there. They want her to hear what they say and they want her to know they are involved in the green revolution, and that includes veganism and love of animals and the environment. Greta's arrival in America may be the most important thing to happen here ever. It will be gigantic. Teens marching and protesting and demanding an improvement in the environment. It can be done. Will take some sacrifice and a lot of effort, but this planet can be saved.

Be careful Greta. America has many crazies walking around free. They are often armed and full of hatred, especially if they see you as a threat to their own little worlds and they don't understand your message. There are a lot of people like that. Ignorant and dangerous. It only takes one at the wrong time and place.

12. Greta's Former Speeches

Greta speaks to UN Secretary general Antonio Guterres in Katowice, Poland

For 25 years countless of people have stood in front of the United Nations climate conferences, asking our nations leaders to stop the emissions. But, clearly this has not worked since the emissions just continue to rise.

So I will not ask them anything.

Instead I will ask the media to start treating the crisis as a crisis.

Instead I will ask the people around the world to realize that our political leaders have failed us.

Because we are facing an existential threat and there is no time to continue down this road of madness.

Rich countries like Sweden need to start reducing emissions by at least 15% every year to reach the 2 degree warming target. You would think the media and everyone of our leaders would be talking about nothing else – but no one ever even mentions it.

Nor does hardly anyone ever talk about that we are in the midst of the sixth mass extinction, with up to 200 species going extinct every single day.

Furthermore does no one ever speak about the aspect of equity clearly stated everywhere in the Parisagreement, which is absolutely necessary to make it work on a global scale. That means that rich countries like mine need to get down to zero emissions, within 6–12 years with todays emission speed, so that people in poorer countries can highten their standard of living by building some of the infrastructure that we have already built. Such as hospitals, electricity and clean drinking water.

Because how can we expect countries like India, Colombia or Nigeria to care about the climate crisis if we, who already have everything, don't care even a second about our actual commitments to the Paris agreement?

So when school started in August this year I sat myself down on the ground outside the Swedish parliament. I school striked for the climate.

Some people say that I should be in school instead. Some people say that I should study to become a climate scientist so that I can "solve the climate crisis". But the climate crisis has already been solved. We already have all the facts and solutions.

And why should I be studying for a future that soon may be no more, when no one is doing anything to save that future? And what is the point of learning facts when the most important facts clearly means nothing to our society?

Today we use 100 million barrels of oil every single day. There are no politics to change that. There are no rules to keep that oil in the ground.

So we can't save the world by playing by the rules. Because the rules have to be changed.

So we have not come here to beg the world leaders to care for our future. They have ignored us in the past and they will ignore us again.

We have come here to let them know that change is coming whether they like it or not. The people will rise to the challenge. And since our leaders are behaving like children, we will have to take the responsibility they should have taken long ago.

Thank You!

Greta Speaks at the World Economic Forum, Davos, Switzerland

Our house is on fire, I am here to say our house is on fire. According to the IPCC we are less than 12 years away from not being able to undo our mistakes.

In that time unprecedented changes in all aspects of society needs to have taken place including a reduction of our co2 emissions by at least 50% and please note that those numbers do not include the aspect of equity which is absolutely necessary to make the Paris agreement work on a global scale. Nor does it include tipping points or feedback loops like the extreme powerful methane gas being released from the thawing Arctic permafrost.

At places like Davos people like to tell success stories but their financial success has come with an unthinkable price tag. And on climate change we have to acknowledge that we have failed. All political movements in their present form have done so. And the media has failed to create broad public awareness. But Homo sapiens have not yet failed. Yes we are failing but there is still time to turn everything around we can still fix this, we still have everything in our own hands. But unless we recognize the overall failures of our current systems we must probably those probably don't stand a chance.

We are facing a disaster of unspoken sufferings for enormous amounts of people and now is not the time for speaking politely, we're focusing on what we can or cannot say. Now it's the time to speak clearly. Solving the client crisis is the greatest and most complex challenge that Homo sapiens has have ever faced.

The main solution however is so simple that even a small child can understand it. We have to stop the emissions of greenhouse gases. And either we do that or we don't. You say nothing in life is black or white but that is a lie, a very dangerous lie. Either we prevent a 1.5 degree of warming or we don't. Either we avoid setting off that irreversible chain reaction beyond the human control, or we don't. Either we choose to go on as a civilization or we don't. That is as black or white as it gets.

There are no gray areas when it comes to survival. Now we all have a choice. We can create transformational action that will safeguard the future living conditions for humankind, or we can continue with our business as usual and fail. That is up to you and me.

Some say that we should not engage in activism, instead we should leave everything to our politicians and just vote for change instead. But what do we do when there is no political will? What do we do when the politics needn't are nowhere in sight?

Here in Davos, just like everywhere else, everyone is talking about money. It seems that money and growth are our only main concerns. And since the climate crisis is a crisis that has never once been treated as a crisis, people are simply not aware of the full consequences of our everyday life.

People are not aware that there is such a thing as a carbon budget, and just how incredible small that remaining carbon budget is. And that needs to change today. No other current challenge can match the importance of establishing a wide public awareness and understanding of our rapidly disappearing carbon budgets that should and must become a new global currency in the very heart of future and present economics.

We are now at a time in history where everyone with any insight of the climate crisis that threatens our civilization and the entire biosphere must speak out in clear language, no matter how uncomfortable and unprofitable that may be. We must change almost everything in our current societies. The bigger your carbon footprint is, the bigger your moral duty. The bigger your platform the bigger your responsibility.

Adults keep saying we owe it to the young people to give them hope. But I don't want your hope, I don't want you to be hopeful. I want you to panic, I want you to feel the fear I feel every day. And then I want you to act, I want you to act as if you would in a crisis. I want you to act as if the house was on fire, because it is.

Some people say that we are not doing enough to fight climate change. But that is not true. Because to "not do enough" you have to do something. And the truth is we are basically not doing anything.

Yes, some people are doing more than they can but they are too few or too far away from power to make a difference today.

Some people say that the climate crisis is something that we all have created. But that is just another convenient lie. Because if everyone is guilty then no one is to blame.

And someone is to blame. Some people - some companies and some decision m akers in particular - has known exactly what priceless values they are sacrificing to continue making unimaginable amounts of money.

I want to challenge those companies and those decision makers into real and bold climate action. To set their economic goals aside and to safeguard the future living conditions for human kind.

I don't believe for one secondthat you will rise to that challenge. But I want to ask you all the same.

I ask you to prove me wrong. For the sake of your children, for the sake of your grandchildren. For the sake of life and this beautiful living planet.

I ask you to stand on the right side of history. I ask you to pledge to do everything in your power to push your own business or government in line with a 1.5 degree world.

Will you pledge to do that? Will you pledge to join me, and the people all around the world in doing whatever it takes.

Greta Speaks at the National Assembly in Paris

I have some good news and some bad news regarding the planet's emergency. I will start with the good news. The world will not end in 11 years as some people have been saying. The bad news however, in the year 2030 if we go on with business as usual, there may be a number of tipping points and we might not be able to undo the irreversible climate changes.

There are a number of people who do not agree with what we are saying. They say we are children and exaggerate things. They say we are alarmists, but at current consumption levels our carbon dioxide budget will be expended in 8 and ½ years. I have never heard even once any politician or business leader mention the danger we are in. We children have to become the bad guys and tell people about the climate crisis because our leaders will not do it. Maybe they just do not understand.

I and other leaders of the youth environmental movement are hated and scorned. We are lied to and ignored by the politicians. There is no middle ground when it comes to the climate emergency. The richer countries must act faster and the poor countries need extra time to improve their infrastructure such as roads, water, schools, hospitals, and bridges. The media has ignored the science and that is why the people do not know what is happening.

You cannot solve the crisis without seeing the whole picture. You cannot leave the responsibility for the preservation of this planet to politicians and expect them to take action. This has to be for everything and everyone. Our carbon dioxide budget is painfully small and you must realize that hardly anything is being done about it and most people do not even realize that it exists.

Tell me exactly what you do and how do you do it without funding. Those are the questions we must ask ourselves and ask our leaders. The science is clear and all of us children are viewing and acting upon that science. Politicians who say they ae acting upon it are probably doing more harm than good because no real change is in sight. The worst danger is not our inaction, it is when the politicians list all the things that are being done when nothing is being done.

Some people have chosen not to come here today. They don't want to listen to us because after all, we are just children and they do not have to listen to us. But they do have to listen to the united science. That is all we ask. Unite behind the science.

Greta's Speech in Stockholm

When I was about eight years old, I first heard about something called climate change or global warming. Apparently, that was something humans have created by our way of living. I was told to turn off the lights to save energy and to recycle paper to save resources. I remember thinking that it was very strange that humans, who are an animal species among others, could be capable of changing the Earth's climate. Because if we were, and if it was really happening, we wouldn't be talking about anything else. As soon as you'd turn on the TV, everything would be about that. Headlines, radio, newspapers, you would never read or hear about anything else, as if there was a world war going on. But no one ever talked about it.

If burning fossil fuels was so bad that it threatened our very existence, how could we just continue like before? Why were there no restrictions? Why wasn't it made illegal? To me, that did not add up. It was too unreal. So when I was 11, I became ill. I fell into depression, I stopped talking, and I stopped eating. In two months, I lost about 10 kilos of weight.

Later on, I was diagnosed with Asperger syndrome, OCD and selective mutism. That basically means I only speak when I think it's necessary - now is one of those moments. (Applause) For those of us who are on the spectrum, almost everything is black or white. We aren't very good at lying, and we usually don't enjoy participating in this social game that the rest of you seem so fond of. (Laughter) I think in many ways that we autistic are the normal ones, and the rest of the people are pretty strange, (Laughter) especially when it comes to the sustainability crisis, where everyone keeps saying climate change is an existential threat and the most important issue of all, and yet they just carry on like before. I don't understand that, because if the emissions have to stop, then we must stop the emissions.

To me that is black or white. There are no gray areas when it comes to survival. Either we go on as a civilization or we don't. We have to change. Rich countries like Sweden need to start reducing emissions by at least 15 percent every year. And that is so that we can stay below a two-degree warming target. Yet, as the IPCC have recently demonstrated, aiming instead for 1.5 degrees Celsius would significantly reduce the climate impacts.

But we can only imagine what that means for reducing emissions. You would think the media and every one of our leaders would be talking about nothing else, but they never even mention it. Nor does anyone ever mention the greenhouse gases already locked in the system. Nor that air pollution is hiding a warming so that when we stop burning fossil fuels, we already have an extra level of warming perhaps as high as 0.5 to 1.1 degrees Celsius. Furthermore does hardly anyone speak about the fact that we are in the midst of the sixth mass extinction, with up to 200 species going extinct every single day, that the extinction rate today is between 1,000 and 10,000 times higher than what is seen as normal.

Nor does hardly anyone ever speak about the aspect of equity or climate justice, clearly stated everywhere in the Paris Agreement, which is absolutely necessary to make it work on a global scale. That means that rich countries need to get down to zero emissions within 6 to 12 years, with today's emission speed. And that is so that people in poorer countries can have a chance to heighten their standard of living by building some of the infrastructure that we have already built, such as roads, schools, hospitals, clean drinking water, electricity, and so on. Because how can we expect countries like India or Nigeria to care about the climate crisis if we who already have everything don't care even a second about it or our actual commitments to the Paris Agreement?

So, why are we not reducing our emissions? Why are they in fact still increasing? Are we knowingly causing a mass extinction? Are we evil? No, of course not. People keep doing what they do because the vast majority doesn't have a clue about the actual consequences of our everyday life, and they don't know that rapid change is required. We all think we know, and we all think everybody knows, but we don't. Because how could we? If there really was a crisis, and if this crisis was caused by our emissions, you would at least see some signs.

Not just flooded cities, tens of thousands of dead people, and whole nations leveled to piles of torn down buildings. You would see some restrictions. But no. And no one talks about it. There are no emergency meetings, no headlines, no breaking news. No one is acting as if we were in a crisis. Even most climate scientists or green politicians keep on flying around the world, eating meat and dairy. If I live to be 100, I will be alive in the year 2103.

When you think about the future today, you don't think beyond the year 2050. By then, I will, in the best case, not even have lived half of my life. What happens next? The year 2078, I will celebrate my 75th birthday. If I have children or grandchildren, maybe they will spend that day with me. Maybe they will ask me about you, the people who were around, back in 2018. Maybe they will ask why you didn't do anything while there still was time to act. What we do or don't do right now will affect my entire life and the lives of my children and grandchildren.

What we do or don't do right now, me and my generation can't undo in the future. So when school started in August of this year, I decided that this was enough. I set myself down on the ground outside the Swedish parliament. I school striked for the climate. Some people say that I should be in school instead. Some people say that I should study to become a climate scientist so that I can "solve the climate crisis."

But the climate crisis has already been solved. We already have all the facts and solutions. All we have to do is to wake up and change. And why should I be studying for a future that soon will be no more when no one is doing anything whatsoever to save that future? And what is the point of learning facts in the school system when the most important facts given by the finest science of that same school system clearly means nothing to our politicians and our society. Some people say that Sweden is just a small country, and that it doesn't matter what we do, but I think that if a few children can get headlines all over the world just by not coming to school for a few weeks, imagine what we could all do together if you wanted to. (Applause)

Now we're almost at the end of my talk, and this is where people usually start talking about hope, solar panels, wind power, circular economy, and so on, but I'm not going to do that. We've had 30 years of pep-talking and selling positive ideas. And I'm sorry, but it doesn't work. Because if it would have, the emissions would have gone down by now. They haven't.

And yes, we do need hope, of course we do. But the one thing we need more than hope is action. Once we start to act, hope is everywhere. So instead of looking for hope, look for action. Then, and only then, hope will come. Today, we use 100 million barrels of oil every single day. There are no politics to change that. There are no rules to keep that oil in the ground. So we can't save the world by playing by the rules, because the rules have to be changed. Everything needs to change, and it has to start today. Thank you. (Applause)

13. Greta's speech to Parliament in London.

My name is Greta Thunberg. I am 16 years old. I come from Sweden. And I speak on behalf of future generations.

I know many of you don't want to listen to us – you say we are just children. But we're only repeating the message of the united climate science.

Many of you appear concerned that we are wasting valuable lesson time, but I assure you we will go back to school the moment you start listening to science and give us a future. Is that really too much to ask?

In the year 2030 I will be 26 years old. My little sister Beata will be 23. Just like many of your own children or grandchildren. That is a great age, we have been told. When you have all of your life ahead of you. But I am not so sure it will be that great for us.

I was fortunate to be born in a time and place where everyone told us to dream big; I could become whatever I wanted to. I could live wherever I wanted to. People like me had everything we needed and more. Things our grandparents could not even dream of. We had everything we could ever wish for and yet now we may have nothing.

Now we probably don't even have a future any more.

Because that future was sold so that a small number of people could make unimaginable amounts of money. It was stolen from us every time you said that the sky was the limit, and that you only live once.

You lied to us. You gave us false hope. You told us that the future was something to look forward to. And the saddest thing is that most children are not even aware of the fate that awaits us. We will not understand it until it's too late. And yet we are the lucky ones. Those who will be affected the hardest are already suffering the consequences. But their voices are not heard.

Around the year 2030, 10 years 252 days and 10 hours away from now, we will be in a position where we set off an irreversible chain reaction beyond human control, that will most likely lead to the end of our civilization as we know it. That is unless in that time, permanent and unprecedented changes in all aspects of society have taken place, including a reduction of CO_2 emissions by at least 50%

And please note that these calculations are depending on inventions that have not yet been invented at scale, inventions that are supposed to clear the atmosphere of astronomical amounts of carbon dioxide.

Furthermore, these calculations do not include unforeseen tipping points and feedback loops like the extremely powerful methane gas escaping from rapidly thawing arctic permafrost.

Nor do these scientific calculations include already locked-in warming hidden by toxic air pollution. Nor the aspect of equity – or climate justice – clearly stated throughout the Paris agreement, which is absolutely necessary to make it work on a global scale.

We must also bear in mind that these are just calculations. Estimations. That means that these "points of no return" may occur a bit sooner or later than 2030. No one can know for sure. We can, however, be certain that they will occur approximately in these timeframes, because these calculations are not opinions or wild guesses. These projections are backed up by scientific facts, concluded by all nations through the IPCC. Nearly every single major national scientific body around the world unreservedly supports the work and findings of the IPCC.

Did you hear what I just said? Is my English OK? Is the microphone on? Because I'm beginning to wonder. During the last six months I have travelled around Europe for hundreds of hours in trains, electric cars and buses, repeating these life-changing words over and over again. But no one seems to be talking about it, and nothing has changed. In fact, the emissions are still rising.

When I have been travelling around to speak in different countries, I am always offered help to write about the specific climate policies in specific countries. But that is not really necessary. Because the basic problem is the same everywhere. And the basic problem is that basically nothing is being done to halt – or even slow – climate and ecological breakdown, despite all the beautiful words and promises.

The UK is, however, very special. Not only for its mind-blowing historical carbon debt, but also for its current, very creative, carbon accounting.

Since 1990 the UK has achieved a 37% reduction of its territorial CO_2 emissions, according to the Global Carbon Project. And that does sound very impressive. But these numbers do not include emissions from aviation, shipping and those associated with imports and exports. If these numbers are included the reduction is around 10% since 1990 – or an an average of 0.4% a year, according to Tyndall Manchester.

And the main reason for this reduction is not a consequence of climate policies, but rather a 2001 EU directive on air quality that essentially forced the UK to close down its very old and extremely dirty coal power plants and replace them with less dirty gas power stations. And switching from one disastrous energy source to a slightly less disastrous one will of course result in a lowering of emissions.

But perhaps the most dangerous misconception about the climate crisis is that we have to "lower" our emissions. Because that is far from enough. Our emissions have to stop if we are to stay below 1.5-2C of warming. The "lowering of emissions" is of course necessary but it is only the beginning of a fast process that must lead to a stop within a couple of decades, or less. And by "stop" I mean net zero – and then quickly on to negative figures. That rules out most of today's politics.

The fact that we are speaking of "lowering" instead of "stopping" emissions is perhaps the greatest force behind the continuing business as usual. The UK's active current support of new exploitation of fossil fuels – for example, the UK shale gas fracking industry, the expansion of its North Sea oil and gas fields, the expansion of airports as well as the planning permission for a brand new coal mine – is beyond absurd.

This ongoing irresponsible behaviour will no doubt be remembered in history as one of the greatest failures of humankind.

People always tell me and the other millions of school strikers that we should be proud of ourselves for what we have accomplished. But the only thing that we need to look at is the emission curve. And I'm sorry, but it's still rising. That curve is the only thing we should look at.

Every time we make a decision we should ask ourselves; how will this decision affect that curve? We should no longer measure our wealth and success in the graph that shows economic growth, but in the curve that shows the emissions of greenhouse gases. We should no longer only ask: "Have we got enough money to go through with this?" but also: "Have we got enough of the carbon budget to spare to go through with this?" That should and must become the centre of our new currency.

Many people say that we don't have any solutions to the climate crisis. And they are right. Because how could we? How do you "solve" the greatest crisis that humanity has ever faced? How do you "solve" a war? How do you "solve" going to the moon for the first time? How do you "solve" inventing new inventions?

The climate crisis is both the easiest and the hardest issue we have ever faced. The easiest because we know what we must do. We must stop the emissions of greenhouse gases. The hardest because our current economics are still totally dependent on burning fossil fuels, and thereby destroying ecosystems in order to create everlasting economic growth.

"So, exactly how do we solve that?" you ask us – the schoolchildren striking for the climate. And we say: "No one knows for sure. But we have to stop burning fossil fuels and restore nature and many other things that we may not have quite figured out yet."

Then you say: "That's not an answer!"

So we say: "We have to start treating the crisis like a crisis – and act even if we don't have all the solutions."

"That's still not an answer," you say.

Then we start talking about circular economy and rewilding nature and the need for a just transition. Then you don't understand what we are talking about.

We say that all those solutions needed are not known to anyone and therefore we must unite behind the science and find them together along the way. But you do not listen to that. Because those answers are for solving a crisis that most of you don't even fully understand. Or don't want to understand.

You don't listen to the science because you are only interested in solutions that will enable you to carry on like before. Like now. And those answers don't exist anymore. Because you did not act in time.

Avoiding climate breakdown will require cathedral thinking. We must lay the foundation while we may not know exactly how to build the ceiling.

Sometimes we just simply have to find a way. The moment we decide to fulfil something, we can do anything. And I'm sure that the moment we start behaving as if we were in an emergency, we can avoid climate and ecological catastrophe. Humans are very adaptable: we can still fix this. But the opportunity to do so will not last for long. We must start today. We have no more excuses.

We children are not sacrificing our education and our childhood for you to tell us what you consider is politically possible in the society that you have created. We have not taken to the streets for you to take selfies with us, and tell us that you really admire what we do.

We children are doing this to wake the adults up. We children are doing this for you to put your differences aside and start acting as you would in a crisis. We children are doing this because we want our hopes and dreams back. I hope my microphone was on. I hope you could all hear

Internet comments to Greta

Michelle Levenson Southard People like you need to stop using her Aspergers as an excuse to tear her down. Instead of seeing it as a disability, she has turned it into an asset. She says things like they are rather than dancing around the subject like most adults. She knows our planet doesn't have time for this. She isn't jet setting around either. The sailors that you mentioned that have to fly to the US to bring the boat home, had to do this because of the short notice they got and are offsetting their carbon footprint by donating to environmental causes. The 4 million dollar boat you refer to is also a research vessel. Boris has teamed up with scientists to turn his boat into a floating lab. They are taking samples of the water while they sail. It is not a luxury liner! This site is for people to SUSTAIN Greta not tear her down. Grow up and try to support someone who is doing the right thing. You sound jealous of her ability to inspire others. I feel sorry for you that you can't see the good she is doing. Many people are doing amazing things for our planet and should be applauded, but we all can't be Greta and have her opportunities. We just have to support her and do what we can for our part in saving our planet.

Carmine Lake Martin Hutchinson She looks pretty healthy to me! She is doing a great job, she got your attention didn't she, she has got you thinking and talking about it.

Mijanou Sutcliffe Carmine Lake : agree! These pontificators, sour grapes narrow minded individuals are part of the problem. We need to look ahead and many of the solutions are there already and can be implemented. It needs momentum and Greta has done it! Standing up for Nature is a Noble Cause❤️⬛gold for all I care. She is worth it! What is your problem

Ina Davies What a beginning of your sabbatical year, sailing across the Atlantic ocean! And see land for the first time after 15 days. Your dedication for climate change is amazing. Both with words and actions. Hope people will listen to you there.

Catherine Cheyne Well done! I'm sure a hot shower and a comfortable bed will be welcome. But of course there is still much work ahead and we are all supporting you! Thanks to the crew for allowing you this incredible opportunity and for getting you safely across the Atlantic ⬛

Johanna Powell Happy to know you had a safe journey. The hearts of many have travelled with you! I am looking forward to hearing your progress on this side of the Atlantic!

Udo Schewietzek Hey New York, give her and the crew a nice and warm welcome.

Greta Thunberg August 25

Strong winds are pushing us west. We expect to arrive at North Cove Marina in Manhattan, New York sometime Tuesday afternoon or evening.

Jenn Lee My little girl (5 years old) and I have been following you on this trip and before! You are an amazing young lady and we are soooo proud of you! Thank you Greta! ❤️⍰❤️⍰❤️⍰⍰⍰⍰⍰⍰

Melissa Bryner Mark I've been following your course on a map in my home office. You're a lot braver than I was at your age. You're also more awake to what is happening to our planet. I'm so grateful for you and those who support you.

Georgina Garon I love following your journey all the way from New Zealand Greta. You are such an inspiration to so many of us.

Reed Robertson Not New Zealand......

Sailor Mare Be very proud of your decision to sail across the Atlantic. That's quite a feat for anyone!! Well done!! You will be happy to see land and a normal bed and bathroom soon.

Gina Nezil Awesome Greta! You go make it happen girl! You represent us, the majority of humans here and now and we are behind you. Sadly, our house is literally on fire. We need to come together now. I am so proud of you dear Greta!

Mel Bee I've raced a sailboat in that weather Greta, and it can certainly be a scary thing. You are in incredible hands and I'm so honored that you are making this journey to our country. You're quite the sea goddess out there- thank you for the frequent updates, it's such a blessing to watch your journey! ⛵

Claire Denney-Price Such an inspirational young lady, I teach my daughters about you and show them all you are doing for our planet. Keep going and thank you ❤

Amy Goldman Koss I'm thrilled to learn such a boat exists! Thanks to those who built and are building it! And thanks for telling us it exists, Greta. I so appreciate you helping us see!

Greta Thunberg

August 22 at 8:12 AM •

Even out here in the middle of the Atlantic Ocean I hear about the record amount of devastating fires in the Amazon.

My thoughts are with those affected. Our war against nature must end.

Victoria Garafola Greta please use your voice to educate people on the connection between these fires and the beef industry. The fires were started intentionally by ranchers to clear their land to grow crops of their livestock. Although I'd love for everyone to commit

Martina Bjorkenor Fernandes Thank you for helping shine a spotlight on this catastrophe. With the rainforest producing 20% of our oxygen, as well as representing enormous biodiversity, I wish there was a way for all governments to step in and take a joint approach to safeguard these amazing eco systems

Greta Thunberg

@gretathunbergsweden

United Nations is at North Cove Marina, NYC.Like Page

August 28 at 7:54 PM • New York, NY •

"We need to stand together and support each other and take action - because otherwise it might be too late."

Welcome to New York Greta Thunberg! We look forward to seeing Greta and other young people from around the world at the UN for next month's Youth #ClimateAction Summit.

Powerful voice of truth to power. Courage of convictions combined with brilliant intellect

Wonderful courageous and smart young person. She rocks!!!!

your a good person strong goals dont worry about the other people live your life for you , everyone ..

Greta Thunberg

August 28 at 6:25 PM •

Finally here. Thank you everyone who came to see me off in Plymouth, and everyone who welcomed me in New York! Now I'm going to rest for a few days, and on Friday I'm going to participate in the strike outside the UN.

Robert Burns Plymouth to around New York (the mouth of the Hudson River, IIRC) is the trip the Pilgrims on the Mayflower intended to make, until they got blown off course to Cape Cod. Interesting

Greta Thunberg

August 28 at 1:23 PM •

Sailing into New York.

We hope that NYC gives you the welcome that you deserve! Most of all, we hope that you get some rest! Loads of ♥⬚ from team ⬚⬚!

Sandra Calderon-Doherty Welcome! I spoke about your arrival today to my college public speaking students in the context of our obligation to speak out in the face of problems and injustice. You are an inspiration! Much love and support from Williamsburg, VA!

Greta Thunberg

August 28 at 8:10 AM •

We have anchored off Coney Island - clearing customs and immigration. We will come ashore at North Cove Marina earliest 14:45 tide allowing.

Robert Burns Careful Greta. If you ever said anything to the effect that we should not allow psychopaths to destroy the Earth through global warming greenhouse gases, CBP will adjudge you as anti-American and deny you a visa.

Rungsrit Kanjanavanit Thank you Neptune for having looking after this extraordinary young lady.

Rungsrit Kanjanavanit Ok thanks both of them.

Greta Thunberg

August 28 at 3:05 AM •

Land!! The lights of Long Island and New York City ahead.

Catherine CheyneCatherine Cheyne Well done! I'm sure a hot shower and a comfortable bed will be welcome. But of course there is still much work ahead and we are all supporting you! Thanks to the crew for allowing you this incredible opportunity and for getting you safely across the Atlantic ⍰

Johanna Powell Happy to know you had a safe journey. The hearts of many have travelled with you! I am looking forward to hearing your progress on this side of the Atlantic!

Udo Schewietzek Hey New York, give her and the crew a nice and warm welcome.

Sarah Benjamins Fantastic, thank you 🙏 and congratulations - I hope you feel invincible after that trip!! Take some time to rest and prepare for the multi sensory assault that is New York. Find a place of refuge where you can rest from all that each day. We're with you in spirit Greta, you amazing human ☺

Anna Lindroth Exciting! I am so looking forward to follow your time in US and hope that you will have a great impact on US politics and make many change their way of living for the good of the climate, all to give our grandchildren a better world to live in

Max Herrera WELCOME TO AMERICA, LITTLE VIKING WARRIOR!

Patricia Saulis Awesome! Its the land of the people who were there before New York! Our relatives the Shinnecock and other tribes. I am sure we are all so glad to see you! ☺❤

John Gardner Must be a magical moment after your days at sea. Congratulations to all the crew.

Let your message be heard from the east coast to the west coast. Together we can save this planet we share.

Marília Breite Wow. You made it girl. I'm so proud of you. You're smart, lovely and brave girl. We love you Greta.

Deb Castellana Almost there! Hope you sail past the Statue of Liberty and get a photo! You are also one such great lady! xo

Randi Probst Greta, you are amazing and really inspiring!!! Thanks for taking this journey for all of us!

Jim Frazier Welcome! Indeed, you are very welcome here and I look forward to hearing your voice for the environment.

Stefaan C. Hublou-Solfrian Ten thousand likes in 32 minutes! 580 written comments. That is the kind of attention this our wonder woman deserves. - With the forest fires going on from Yakutsk in Siberia over Central Africa and Greece, up to Peru, Bolivia and Amazon in Brazilia.... who is the man or woman to doubt the historic role our

Tani Juarez Well done, Greta. Your mission is more important now than ever. I'm an old lady from Pittsburgh and I'm very proud of you.

Stefania Grignani Love Greta!!!!So much Love to you and the crew there!!!Morning all and Morning USA.Love from Italy

Trish Fyock Greta, you're one of my heroes.

I pray you have a wonderful and productive time while on your mission to OPEN THE HEARTS and MINDS of the people to the sufferings of our planet.

Judith Irons Wonderful!! That must look almost strange to you after all this time ☐ I expect the craziness of NYC will take some adjusting to after all the relative solitude and peace. Take very good care Greta xxx

Nani Härkönen That's amazing!! You truly inspire us to make better choices for the environment. <3

Kicki Hermelin Yes!, you made it! Love from Sweden ☐❤

Daisy Lynch So good to see you arriving safely!!

Elsa Salgado Anacleto Welcome to the USA Greta, they say it's "the land of the free and the home of the brave." You'll fit right at home brave girl!

Michael Bresser I hope people hear your message. At the UN and in the whole world. Love from Germany

Matthew Andrews The wonderful symbolism of leaving by boat from Plymouth to New York...probably lost on the people you need to get the message through to...but then a lot is lost to them..

Sarah Luxton Well done Greta! Awesome achievement for someone who's not sailed before and to just head out on a ocean yacht #impressive

Uwe Ramhold You are not on this ship during this trip.Show us please live videos from this trip.German tv morning show ask for you...for the live show....the answer allways...she fall in sleep.This is prediculous.

Gayatri Banerjee Great! Every day I waited for the update from you. I have supported you from the day I came to know about you and your actions. There are lot of climate skeptics around me. I know how difficult it is for a young girl to follow through with her ideas with conviction. Its so great to have the family support you. May you inspire more and more people. God bless you and may you have a succesful stay at US.

Eva-Maria Lohwasser You are an inspiration, I hope the shock of the metropolis after 2 weeks at sea isn't too severe.

Susanne Chakan YEA...I bet it's great to see land after those rough sea waters! Not to mention a shower and real food! WELCOME TO New York...⁇

Nélida A. Flores Fernández Wow! That's a view! You have been so patient and your trip remind me the journeys of so many explorers who challenged the unknown following their dreams. Good luck in "The Big Apple".

Julia Weckman We (me and my kids) have been following your trip from Europe to New York almost every day. The picture shows (interestingly) how nitrogen oxides meet in urban air of New York after the sea. Nitrogen dioxide NO_2 in urban air comes from traffic exhaust

Thea Laurie What an adventure and what a great purpose!

James Cottle Well done to your crew for getting you safely over the pond. And well done you your American Journey is just starting, I look forward to following your journey throughout America North & South.

Claire Williams A massive achievement Greta! What an amazing sight to see! Well done everyone x

Tasja Wohler Wow! So happy you have arrived, been glued to the screen on your epic journey!

Sean O'hAimheirgin Remember, they might appear big and important but you and your message are lifelines to an impoverished and dying country. ❤️☐

Hannah Carter What an amazing achievement and endurance you have undertaken. The world is watching and I do hope listening and learning from your wisdom. Enjoy being on terra firma very soon....

Robbie Marchildon Happy to hear you safely made it to New York! ☐☐☐

Stefaan C. Hublou-Solfrian Aah! We love you. Life is wonderful. Thank God. - Best wishes, I hope you will have a great and enjoyable first day on the American Continent. And in the United States of America. Thanks again for keeping us posted. Kind regards, also to the devoted Sailing Crew and your father.

Mark Hatch An amazing achievement! But with your strength and commitment I am sure your greatest achievements in America are yet to come! I hope you enjoyed your voyage. You inspire us all to try harder.

Youno Erick Welcome to America! Don't mind that guy supposedly in charge.

Daniel Tompkinson Well done Greta you've done an awesome sailing across the Atlantic. You're awesome. Keep up the great work. You've shown the world what you're made of xo.

Cay Chandler Welcome. I am out on Long Island in westhampton, I wish there was a schedule of where you are going to be so I could come see and support you. Waving at you ❤️⁇

Branka Ruzak What an incredible voyage! Welcome to New York ! I am cheering you on as your adventure continues! Best wishes! You are awesome!

Louise Walker Well done Greta!! Thank you for standing above the crowd and making your voice heard!!

Méla Schaus Congrats for this long but successful journey, we are curious to know what will be your programm now and will follow your first steps in the US

Steven Sumerson Almost there. Great journey Greta.

Cally Lee Amazing well done! All the best in New York!

Gilli Paehr You and all them on board have done a great job to show the world what people can do for their conviction. Keep safe and we wish a warm welcome in the USA. You are a great young lady.

Kristoffer Tangri Welcome to New York and good luck!

Karl Fuller You've not travelled until experiencing a landfall after weeks at sea. Go Greta!

Greta Thunberg

August 27 at 7:45 PM •

Home Sweet Home since 14 days. Soon last evening onboard Malizia II.Tomorrow we reach New York.

Gary Slate Thank you for your shining example of love for this beautiful planet! You have captured the attention of the world with your courage and determination!

Scott Gianelli As a New Yorker I say welcome. As a climate scientist I say thank you.

Krista Vander Griend Proud of you for your integrity, tenacity, intelligence and determination! Thank you for being awesome, Greta!

Crys Davis Goodnight darling Greta. You are one amazing young woman! Wishing you the very best in New York. Please keep us updated. You are admired the world over and have inspired us all to be better people in aiding our ailing planet. ♻♥

Paola Romano I teach debate in English and I keep talking about you! Greetings from Buenos Aires. I would love to have you here! Best sweet brave Greta!

Jane Anne Drinkwater May there be a soft warm bed waiting for you , many delicious meals at your command and a huge crowd of people for support. I wish I was there!

Claire Louise Cohen-Norris Welcome to New York, Greta Thunberg! Thank you for your perseverence and dedication and hard work...and for coming to our nation. We are clearly mixed up and confused at the moment, and need clarion calls to moral and ethical action. Thank you for stepping up to fill the void.

Robert Conrad Thank you for sharing your journey with us Greta and all that you have done since the beginning of your journey :) Reading this as I kayak into the sunset. Best of luck in New York ;)

Rune Ahlström I've got nothing but respect for you Greta. Respect and love. What a way to take a year off school. Whatever happens in the year ahead I have no doubt you will think the time was well spent when you look back at it afterwards. What an experience it must be. Do I need to say I am proud to be a swede? ⍰

Donna Kay What a great adventure this has been, Greta, I predict the first of many! Welcome to the U.S.A.!

Milca Van Den Steene That was a beautiful home sweet home.. i guess you'll be sad to say goodbye to the beautiful people you've shared such incredible precious time with.. so grateful they have supported you by sailing you accross the Atlantic ocean.. much LOVE to all of you!

Katherine De George Thank you for inspiring us, Greta - and for being a beacon of light and clarity. You were made for the times we are living in and I am deeply grateful for your leadership.

Flora June McCoy Loads of respect and admiration to you! I'm hoping you and those you lead will save our planet. Thank you for trying.

Kathy Mallett Peters Wishing I were back in my home town of NY right now to welcome you when you arrive. WE NEED YOU in the U.S.!!!!! I want you to bring your passion to our youth~!!!!

Christian Lohberger Well done for such an epic voyage and inspiring so many of us to find alternatives to flying.

Rungsrit Kanjanavanit Love you ❤️❓

How are you planning your return journey?

Mélanie Benoit Conroy So proud of you and your team! Good luck from Canada!

Kimberly Wallis Greta, I truly believe you are History in the making. You must be exhausted, what a journey!Welcome honey ,and I hope someone captures a picture of your face as the Statue of Liberty welcomes you with open arms!!! God bless you and God Bless Americia. ❓❓❤️❓

Thomas Dorfman Must be hard on you, this trip...A very worthy cause, though! You are very inspiring, and I hope people catch on!

Jeannie Flynn Hope you've enjoyed the trip What an adventure New York!

Cynthia Jurs Wow it seems suddenly very quick that you are there! One day in the midst of rough waters then that speed boat running on the sun and the wind brings you to our shores. Many blessings on the captain and crew and most of all you.

Ashley M Brown Girl, you are going to love the pizza!! Congrats on making it across the pond. We welcome you and can't wait to see you make waves on our soil ❤️

Diana Palmentiero Thank you so much for raising awareness about this world crisis! You are an inspiration for all of us!

Jane Ellen Congratulations on your first ocean voyage! Best wishes for your talks in New York.

Sheila H Craig Welcome to the USA! We're behind you/ with you/ ready to climb this hill and nurture our home. Love to you all!

Leatherhead Martinez We welcome you! Please stay positive thru this visit. Unfortunately , you will encounter so many negative people who will not be to ignorant to open there minds to the gift you bring. They do not speak for the whole of us. Just more eger to make fools of themselves! Thanks again young earth warrior!

Susan Colliton Welcome to America, Greta! Thank you so much for coming and spreading your vitally important message about the climate crisis here. You made a courageous journey across the ocean to help save life on Earth - so inspiring!

Garry Marchand You are such an amazing young woman Greta I wish you all the best and hope that the message you bring will be heard and decisive actions taken.

Jane Gardner Go Greta! All of us at Plan International are cheering for you! You really are an inspiration for girls... we've just received results from a survey of Australian girls and you're they're #1 inspiration - truly.

Suzanne Cheavens There are so many of us who welcome you with open arms, and many who will greet you with skepticism, disdain, even. As you deliver your message, remember those of us who understand that we must believe the science, act now and work toward a healthy future. You are not alone. Welcome!

Erkki Poikolainen I have been looking every day where you go. Safe trip until the end. You are doing great work Greta.

David Utiger I'm sure you know that we have a horrible and illegitimate government that the majority of us do not support. That being said there are millions of us Americans that admire you and are fighting for the causes you believe in. Welcome..

Manuela Campanelli Welcome to the US! I wish we could meet sometimes. An astrophysicist who admires you and support you!

Lenka Mrkvickova Amazing Greta! What an incredible human you are! Thank you for being the light in this world! ☐

Siân Canning Well done! This is an excellent achievement, what an adventure. I am looking forward to learning all about what it has been like. Take care.

Deborah White-Machon The question I've hesitated to ask all day....are you going back that way too? Personally I couldn't do one crossing. You amaze me. I would never hold it against you by flying back. I have anxiety and depression and I see you doing this

Ed Norris I wish you a long, motionless, sound sleep ASAP, Greta! May it come *before* your next big event! You have earned it! :p

Big thanks to your team for getting you here safely!

Ajith Gopi Proud of you Greta. Your epic journey across the atlantic with almost zero fossil fuels will be ever remembered in history as part of the fight against climate change

Franny Langlois Great work Greta I have been posting you to my friends to shake them up a bit and to rise the masses to stop this horrible mess we have done to the world. Love you. Are you speaking in the USA?

Bonnie Davis Be prepared. We may not be who you think we are. There is a different president and his party rides with him. Beware. They do not take kindly to climate or science discussions. Godspeed.

Brian Russ Let us know if you wanna come have dinner with my family in Brooklyn. Serious offer - my wife Lauren and I love you and I'm working on a novel where you are the inspiration for my main character. DM me.

Ed Norris America cries out to unite behind the science. We *must* restore trust that civil servants can lead the way, out of the OILigarchy's grasp. Your message is water to millions of parched palates.

Luke Jobson Amazing effort by all involved! Go blow them away with your trademark wit and authentic love for the planet. Thank you for speaking for those of us who can't ❤️🉑❤️🉑

Michael Keylock Amazing let's hope some of our determination and love for this beautiful planet rubs off where ever you go

Hope Alexander It's been a privilege watching you cross, Greta. Thank you for trying to save us from ourselves.

Peter Bennett Stay safe, enjoy dry land, you will wobble a bit, but it will go away in a day. Love and support from Nova Scotia Canada

Billy McKirdy I hope you will inspire millions of your generation to take control of the narrative and effect that change, the worlds hopes rest on all of your shoulders Greta 🤙 🙂

Patricia Salinas Dear Greta, please come to South America! The Amazon is on fire.

Justine Wilson What an adventure! Wishing you all the best in New York and beyond! ❤️🙂🤙🙂🙂

Greta Thunberg

August 27 at 2:30 PM

Day 14. 119 miles from Manhattan. Very light winds south of Long Island.

Robert Burns If worst comes to worst, you could just take the Long Island Railroad now.

Barbara Kalwaitis There you are! So glad to hear from you, Greta. Welcome to you all! I have gotten used to the daily updates and seeing your face or your shipmate's in the morning. I check the tracker daily to see your location and that's how I start my day. Looking fo...See More

Greta Thunberg

August 26 at 10:40 AM •

Day 13. Rough seas south of Nova Scotia. But conditions closer to New York will be slower than predicted and weather update suggests Wednesday arrival - an updated ETA will come as we near the coast.

Mel Bee I've raced a sailboat in that weather Greta, and it can certainly be a scary thing. You are in incredible hands and I'm so honored that you are making this journey to our country. You're quite the sea goddess out there- thank you for the frequent updates, it's such a blessing to watch your journey! ⛵️

Sandy Blaine Be safe, Greta and crew! What an amazing journey, how wonderful you're almost here. You are an inspiration and a light.

Greta Thunberg

August 25 at 4:50 PM

Strong winds are pushing us west. We expect to arrive at North Cove Marina in Manhattan, New York sometime Tuesday afternoon or evening.

Jenn Lee My little girl (5 years old) and I have been following you on this trip and before! You are an amazing young lady and we are soooo proud of you! Thank you Greta! ❤️❓❤️❓❤️❓❓❓❓❓❓

Melissa Bryner Mark I've been following your course on a map in my home office. You're a lot braver than I was at your age. You're also more awake to what is happening to our planet. I'm so grateful for you and those who support you.

Greta Thunberg

August 25 at 10:29 AM

Day 12. We are getting closer to the North American mainland. Rough conditions, but downwind sailing.

Michel D. Gagné Cm As Joseph Campbell has said: "We must be willing to let go of the life we planned so as to have the life that is waiting for us. A hero is someone who has given his or her life to something bigger than oneself." :-)

Greta Thunberg is one of the new heroes of the 21st century. This is just the beginning of her adventure.

Michelle Levenson Southard Glad to see you so close to our shores! You are an inspiration and we can't wait until you dock in New York! I so wish I could be there to greet you but will be there in spirit! Thank you to the crew for all that they are doing, keeping you safe and for posting your trip on instagram!

Greta Thunberg

August 24 at 12:59 PM

Day 11. Very bumpy and wet, south of Newfoundland.

Mike Mermin Keep up the great work, Greta! We need your voice on this side of the pond, now more than ever. Onward in good health and safe waters!

Patricia Care Hello from Newfoundland! You are an awesome human and keep up the great work!

Greta Thunberg

August 23 at 3:13 PM

school strike week 53.

#fridaysforfuture #climatestrike#schoolstrike4climate

Robert Börjes Awesome. Strike from school, never from learning! Keep up... ⁇

Ahmed Magdy U lost so much weight Greta! Take care of ur self plz

Greta Thunberg

August 22 at 12:26 PM •

Malizia 2 is fitted with solar panels and hydro generators making it one of the very few ships in the world allowing trips like this to be emission free.

Malizia 2 also has an onboard lab to measure ocean surface CO_2 and water temperature in cooperation with Max Planck institute.

Claire Denney-Price Such an inspirational young lady, I teach my daughters about you and show them all you are doing for our planet. Keep going and thank you ❤

Amy Goldman Koss I'm thrilled to learn such a boat exists! Thanks to those who built and are building it! And thanks for telling us it exists, Greta. I so appreciate you helping us see!

Greta Thunberg

August 22 at 8:12 AM •

Even out here in the middle of the Atlantic Ocean I hear about the record amount of devastating fires in the Amazon. My thoughts are with those affected. Our war against nature must end.

Victoria Garafola Greta please use your voice to educate people on the connection between these fires and the beef industry. The fires were started intentionally by ranchers to clear their land to grow crops of their livestock. Although I'd love for everyone to commit t...See More

Martina Bjorkenor Fernandes Thank you for helping shine a spotlight on this catastrophe. With the rainforest producing 20% of our oxygen, as well as representing enormous biodiversity, I wish there was a way for all governments to step in and take a joint approach to safeguard these amazing eco systems.

David Williams As a 67 year old great grandfather I feel ashamed to be a part of the plastic population, although we did not know at the time that plastic would cause do much damage..

All we thought was that it is a great invention.

Please can you accept my own apology.

Catriona Talbot Of course we will never win in a war against nature. And so we are all affected. What is happening is so all- encompassing that our languages can hardly express it. Thank you so much for the amazing work you are doing. You are getting the world's attention and focussing it on the climate crisis in a way that has not been done before. So much respect from this senior citizen.

Eamonn Coyle Hello Greta.

You are doing great work. You are an inspiration. The next Rossa Parks. You have innate leadership skills.

Luz Maria Calvo I live in Bolivia ⬜⬜ 500.000 hectares have been devastated with fire. They say it will take 200 years for the flora and fauna to recover. It is a tragedy for humanity, our lungs are dying! ⬜⬜⬜⬜⬜⬜

Debbie Yuzwa Yes it has too! Thank You Greta for acknowledging the Amazon. My heart is breaking and I'm so proud of what you do and stand for!!!

Marcos Marcos Please help us protest in Brazil against the president Bolsonaro. The world needs to know about this. This is what our sky looks like at 2 p.m. after the smoke form the forest burning reaches the city..

Marlena Baxter I absolutely agree. I stand with you. Since I was a child, I've seen the grace and potential of out home, planet earth. I knew then, that the revolution is an informed, calm elevation, and a graceful turn around.

Christopher Daryl Santos I agree we need to stop the war with nature and start the one FOR NATURE. Not with violence but with enlightenment and awareness. You are one of the precious flames that is making it happen

Joanne McGarry Grieving the Amazon fires and the Arctic ice melt and again asked my city council last night to declare a climate emergency. I also told them about the global strikes in September and that I had invited you to our Northern California redwood forest on your way to Chile. I write this to you in the middle of the Atlantic on your ninth day of travel.

May Pierre win the Navigator Trophy. Peace and all good, Greta.

Alberto Roberto Devastation must end! In the Amazon as well as other parts of the planet. I'm sick and tired of this destructive behavior. Thanks Greta for acknowledging this nonsensical behavior!

Jean-François Larose Why such horror ?: We live in a market economy. Brazil is the largest exporter of beef and cattle in the world. Why ? To supply the increasing worldwide demand for beef and cattle then (according to them) they must burn the Amazon forest to have more

Dave Turnbull The rainforest it BURNING. My question is why all able countries are not mobalizing fire fighters and massive equipment to handle this tragedy as best we can.

Véro Rotkopf We cry for all these forests .it is a shame for all of us

James O'toole It's not our war. Its the wealthy. The corporations. Bolsonaro and the big ranchers. The 1%. Its up to the rest of us to stop them.

Judy Stephenson So frightening. Who will stand for us? Governments of the most powerful nations seem to all be in the pockets of big business. We need to start mass global protests to call all our governments to account!

Laurra Howes It's so sad, when Notre dame had the fire they raised almost 1 billion dollars in two days, praying that the same support can be directed to the Amazon ⍰

Wayne Gurney Gather the facts and speak truth to power.

That is what you have been doing and that is what you should continue to do. Bring rainforest destruction up to the UN.

I look forward to your presentation ...

Marly Donaire I have a bigger and profoundly believe on your great cause Greta. How is it so stupid and greedy and Inhumane for a person to cause this huge catastrophic in nature. I wish and hope ,⍰ that everything you do will put into a blessing ⍰ that humanity should once and for all ponder how we could bring a brighter side of our generation.

Athena Sofianou Who else here thinks that Brazil's president is letting the fires go on for so long on purpose ? Who else thinks this was all orchestrated ? We're never getting these trees back , they're gonna be transformed into whatever the government wants in no time

Tracy Hart Davis I take a container each time I walk on my local beach and it gets filled every single time with tiny bits and shreds of plastic, fish hooks, you name it. Thanks, Greta, for sticking to your morals.

Agneta Hansson How come there was more immediate media coverage when Notre Dame in Paris was on fire, than the media coverage of the Amazonas fires? Media wake up!

Rose Hayes Those fires were set to drive indigenous people from their land. It's all about the money.

Eleanor Blackier I heard about it from my Grandson just yesterday. CBC is too busy covering the SNC-Lavalin story (a non-issue In my opinion) to cover anything important like this. Sad.

Dom Claydon-wallace According to sources near... its being burnt on purpose to provide space for beef farmers. 🉑🉑

Kim Alsten Stiansen There is nothing only Norway can do!!! Every country and every nation need to work together

Adriana Bueno Wiborg Thank you Greta, we are with you on this mission, to educate people and fight against greedy politicians who dont care about the future like Bolsonaro.

Michy Bond Its big news here Greta. We seem to be still helpless against the ones who dont want to fall in line with the majority, who want to stop all this. Its madness that's accelerating every month, NOT every Year. Just had a go at Amazon I invest a lot of my monthly income in. They are using NONE recycble Envelopes, which I will not accept, any goods sent in them will be sent back . Consumer power is whats needed here.

Sandra Montez I wonder what some politicians have in their heads. It's true that the money makes the world go around but money is NOT breathable nor eatable!!! What will it take for them to understand that???

Anninha Figueiredo Be by our side, Greta. What is happening here in Brazil is a crime. A huge and terrible crime

Thomas Volkwein Where are the Billionaires from Notre Dame now?

Vincenzo Scognamiglio At ONU assembly, we must ask to recognize, in addition to crimes against humanity, also crimes against nature ...

Silvia Jacon-Bolen There are enough Brazilians fighting against this government! But unfortunately there are enough stupid Brazilians who elected him!!!! He is a horror, worst than every dictator and endless stupid!!!!

David DeShong I am a 50 year old man and you are my hero, Miss. Thank you for your bravery, empathy and for fighting for what is right!

David DeShong Bede Perham --I have heard her speak. I do not "idolize" her but I find her actions heroic. She has her own mind. She is passionate about our planet. Can you support your assertion that she is "brainwashed?" Can you explain how anything she has said is not accurate? The young lady has the courage of her convictions. It sounds to me as if you are threatened by the idea of a future in which women are finally heard.

Bill Lionheart I applaud your choices Greta. I hope you enjoy the trip. Crossing the Atlantic in a sailing boat is a big challenge and you are lucky to have a ride on such a wonderful fast boat. I love that they will change their logos to ones supporting climate action! Is there a link where we can follow your progress across the Atlantic?

Greta Thunberg Yes! you will be able to follow us. I think Ocean Race is doing that for us. I will post the link before we leave the UK.

Martijn Willers Dear Greta, you're a modern day hero, fighting for the most important issue of our time. I'm so impressed by your ideas and actions. Have a safe journey and I hope millions of people will be inspired by you, and will decide to do their bit for a better future of our precious planet earth.

Linda Patterson I am a 70yr old great grandmother. I just wanted you to know how proud I am of you and all of the young people that are fighting to save our planet. I also want to apologize for my generation creating this mess that we have left for your generation. You are the future of our planet.

Greta Thunberg August 21 at 2:18 PM

Day 8. 42° 25' N 39° 27' W. At sea you really lose sense of time and you can't separate the days. You sleep, eat, look at the ocean.

Sandy Blaine Be safe, Greta and crew! What an amazing journey, how wonderful you're almost here. You are an inspiration and a light.

Joanne McGarry Glad to know your arrival is soon. Thank you to your father for joining you on this amazing adventure and I hope the redwoods of Northern California can be a stop on your travels. It would be wonderful to show you this magnificent spot on the planet. I have a friend with a Tesla who can bring you here from the train station.

Sarah Benjamins Fantastic, thank you 🙏 and congratulations - I hope you feel invincible after that trip!! Take some time to rest and prepare for the multi sensory assault that is New York. Find a place of refuge where you can rest from all that each day. We're with you in spirit Greta, you amazing human 💕

Anna Lindroth Exciting! I am so looking forward to follow your time in US and hope that you will have a great impact on US politics and make many change their way of living for the good of the climate, all to give our grandchildren a better world to live in

Max Herrera WELCOME TO AMERICA, LITTLE VIKING WARRIOR!

Patricia Saulis Awesome! Its the land of the people who were there before New York! Our relatives the Shinnecock and other tribes. I am sure we are all so glad to see you! ❤

John Gardner Must be a magical moment after your days at sea. Congratulations to all the crew.

Let your message be heard from the east coast to the west coast. Together we can save this planet we share.

Marília Breite Wow. You made it girl. I'm so proud of you. You're smart, lovely and brave girl. We love you Gret

Deb Castellana Almost there! Hope you sail past the Statue of Liberty and get a photo! You are also one such great lady! Xo

Randi Probst Greta, you are amazing and really inspiring!!! Thanks for taking this journey for all of us!

Jim Frazier Welcome! Indeed, you are very welcome here and I look forward to hearing your voice for the environment.

Stefaan C. Hublolemented. It needs momentum and Greta has done it! Standing up for Nature is a Noble C

Gary Slate Thank you for your shining example of love for this beautiful planet! You have captured the attention of the world with your courage and determination!

Hattie W-s thank you for caring about our planet, our future, and having the courage, grit and determination to do something about it. I'm immensely proud of you!

Scott Gianelli As a New Yorker I say welcome. As a climate scientist I say thank you.

Krista Vander Griend Proud of you for your integrity, tenacity, intelligence and determination! Thank you for being awesome, Greta!

Crys Davis Goodnight darling Greta. You are one amazing young woman! Wishing you the very best in New York. Please keep us updated. You are admired the world over and have inspired us all to be better people in aiding our ailing planet. 🔁🔁🔁🔁🔁🔁🔁🔁🔁♻🔁🔁🔁❤🔁

Paola Romano I teach debate in English and I keep talking about you! Greetings from Buenos Aires. I would love to have you here! Best sweet brave Greta!

Jane Anne Drinkwater May there be a soft warm bed waiting for you , many delicious meals at your command and a huge crowd of people for support. I wish I was there!

Claire Louise Cohen-Norris Welcome to New York, Greta Thunberg! Thank you for your perseverence and dedication and hard work...and for coming to our nation. We are clearly mixed up and confused at the moment, and need clarion calls to moral and ethical action. Thank you for stepping up to fill the void.

Robert Conrad Thank you for sharing your journey with us Greta and all that you have done since the beginning of your journey :)Reading this as I kayak into the sunset. Best of luck in New York ;)

Rune Ahlström I've got nothing but respect for you Greta. Respect and love. What a way to take a year off school. Whatever happens in the year ahead I have no doubt you will think the time was well spent when you look back at it afterwards. What an experience it must be. Do I need to say I am proud to be a swede? ☐

Donna Kay What a great adventure this has been, Greta, I predict the first of many! Welcome to the U.S.A.!

Milca Van Den Steene That was a beautiful home sweet home.. i guess you'll be sad to say goodbye to the beautiful people you've shared such incredible precious time with.. so grateful they have supported you by sailing you accross the Atlantic ocean.. much LOVE to all of you!

Katherine De George Thank you for inspiring us, Greta - and for being a beacon of light and clarity. You were made for the times we are living in and I am deeply grateful for your leadership.

Flora June McCoy Loads of respect and admiration to you! I'm hoping

Kathy Mallett Peters Wishing I were back in my home town of NY right now to welcome you when you arrive. WE NEED YOU in the U.S.!!!!! I want you to bring your passion to our youth~!!!!

Christian Lohberger Well done for such an epic voyage and inspiring so many of us to find alternatives to flying.

Rungsrit Kanjanavanit Love you ❤️⍰

How are you planning your return journey?

Mélanie Benoit Conroy So proud of you and your team! Good luck from Canada!

Kimberly Wallis Greta, I truly believe you are History in the making. You must be exhausted, what a journey! Welcome honey ,and I hope someone captures a picture of your face as the Statue of Liberty welcomes you with open arms!!! God bless you and God Bless America. ⍰⍰♥⍰

Thomas Dorfman Must be hard on you, this trip...A very worthy cause, though! You are very inspiring, and I hope people catch on!

Shelley Jo Welcome to America, and know that many of us see you as a beacon of truth, agree with and believe in your cause.

El Tacoyote I start to believe you're really the " Choose one " , a special and unique human being to awaken conciencies around all over the world .

You represent the future , the hope of young people new generations , the future is yours , but now we all must be involved.

Jeannie Flynn Hope you've enjoyed the trip What an adventure New York!

Cynthia Jurs Wow it seems suddenly very quick that you are there! One day in the midst of rough waters then that speed boat running on the sun and the wind brings you to our shores. Many blessings on the captain and crew and most of all you.

Ashley M Brown Girl, you are going to love the pizza!! Congrats on making it across the pond. We welcome you and can't wait to see you make waves

Printed in Great Britain
by Amazon